Hiking

Gordon Winch & Gregory Blaxell

Illustrated by Jillian Gibson

We hiked in the bush
and saw some wildflowers.

'Look at those wildflowers,'
said Betty Binnum Binnum.

We climbed up a mountain and saw some birds.

'Look at those birds,'
said Betty.

We swam in the river
and saw some ducks.

'Look at those ducks,'
said Betty.

We came to a cave
and saw some bats.

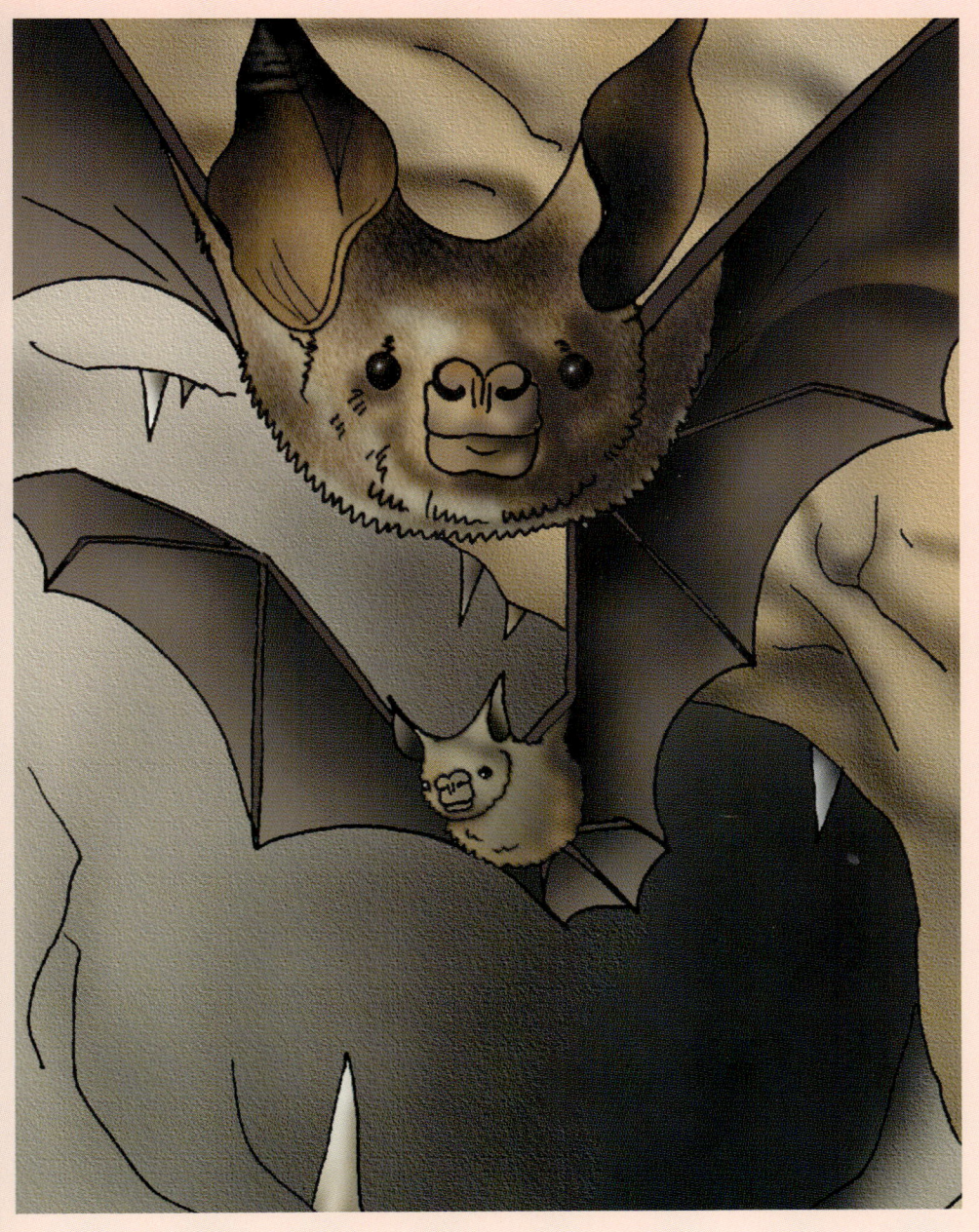

'Look at those bats,'
said Betty.

We looked up at the sky
and saw some stars.

'Look at those stars,'
said Betty.

And then…